# Where Do I Belong?

## Plays About Fitting In

## By Catherine Gourley

CRABTREE
Publishing Company
www.crabtreebooks.com

# Crabtree Publishing Company

**www.crabtreebooks.com**

**Project coordinator:** Kathy Middleton
**Editor:** Reagan Miller
**Proofreader:** Molly Aloian
**Production coordinator:** Ken Wright
**Prepress technician:** Amy Salter
Written, developed, and produced by
RJF Publishing & A+ Media

**Project management:** Julio Abreu,
   Robert Famighetti
**Managing editor:** Mark Sachner
**Associate editor:** Anton Galang
**Design:** Westgraphix LLC/Tammy West
**Illustrations:** Spectrum Creative, Inc.

**Library and Archives Canada Cataloguing in Publication**

Gourley, Catherine, 1950-
   Where do I belong? : plays about fitting in / Catherine Gourley.

(Get into character)
ISBN 978-0-7787-7366-5 (bound).--ISBN 978-0-7787-7380-1 (pbk.)

   1. Self-acceptance--Juvenile drama. 2. Social accept-ance--Juvenile drama. 3. Children's plays, American. I. Title. II. Series: Get into character

PS3557.O86W44 2010     j812'.54     C2009-906783-8

**Library of Congress Cataloging-in-Publication Data**

Gourley, Catherine, 1950-
 Where do I belong? : plays about fitting in / by Catherine Gourley.
   p. cm. -- (Get into character)
 ISBN 978-0-7787-7380-1 (pbk. : alk. paper) -- ISBN 978-0-7787-7366-5 (reinforced library binding : alk. paper)
1. Social acceptance--Juvenile drama. 2. Self-perception--Juvenile drama. 3. Children's plays, American. I. Title.

PS3557.O915W44 2009
812'.6--dc22

2009047085

## Crabtree Publishing Company

www.crabtreebooks.com     1-800-387-7650

Printed in the USA/122009/BG20091103

**Published in Canada**
**Crabtree Publishing**
616 Welland Ave.
St. Catharines, ON
L2M 5V6

**Published in the United States**
**Crabtree Publishing**
PMB 59051
350 Fifth Avenue, 59th Floor
New York, New York 10118

**Published in the United Kingdom**
**Crabtree Publishing**
Maritime House
Basin Road North, Hove
BN41 1WR

**Published in Australia**
**Crabtree Publishing**
386 Mt. Alexander Rd.
Ascot Vale (Melbourne)
VIC 3032

## Series Consultants

**Reading Consultant:** Susan Nations, M.Ed.; Author/Literacy Coach/Consultant in Literacy Development, Sarasota, Florida.

**Content Consultant:** Vinita Bhojwani-Patel, Ph.D.; Certified School/Educational Psychologist, Northfield, Illinois.

# Contents

**Note to the reader:** Be sure to look at the Glossary on page 32 to find definitions of words that might be unfamiliar.

# On the Fringe

When Joe looks at himself in the mirror, he sees an average guy in the ninth grade. He's not the most popular guy in school, but he's never lonely. Things change when Joe tries out for the football team. He discovers a talent he never knew he had—kicking. Making the team as a punter and placekicker shifts Joe from the fringe to the in-crowd. But is life any better for Joe now that he's on the inside?

## Characters:

**Narrators 1, 2, 3**

**Joe Galván**, *a ninth-grade student and bass player*

**Arjun**, *Joe's friend who plays guitar*

**Chelsea**, *Joe's friend who plays drums*

**Coach Barnes**

**Connor Barkley**, *the quarterback*

**Gym teacher**

# Scene 1

**Narrator 1:** It's another ordinary school week for Joe Galván. On Monday, he takes a history test.

**Arjun:** How did you do on the test?

**Joe:** I knew most of the answers. I think I did really well!

**Narrator 2:** On Tuesday, the history teacher returns the tests. Joe's grade is less than what he'd hoped for—a C.

**Narrator 3:** When Joe looks in the mirror, he sees an average guy looking back at him. He's not too tall and not too short. He plays bass guitar, not expertly but not horribly, either. He's not the most popular guy in school—but he does have friends.

**Narrator 1:** This week, however, life is about to change for Joe.

**Narrator 2:** The change begins on Friday in gym class with a game of "punt bowl."

**Arjun:** I hate this game. I always lose. You'll see!

**Joe:** At least it isn't rope climbing. I still have rope burns on my knees from Wednesday. Just once, I'd like to make it to the top.

**Narrator 3:** The teacher divides the class into two teams. Each team takes turns punting a football to the other end of the field.

**Narrator 1:** The punter has to kick the ball inbounds. Otherwise the other team scores a point, and the punter is out. The player who catches the ball has seven seconds to punt the ball, or the kicking team scores a point.

**Narrator 2:** Arjun catches the ball and kicks. The ball sails into the bleachers. As he predicted, he is out of the game.

**Narrator 3:** Off to the side, the football coach hears the gym class cheering and jeering. He strolls over to watch.

**Narrator 1:** The football spirals high, and Joe catches it. The opposing team begins chanting: Seven, six, five, four, three, two—

**Narrator 2:** Joe drops the ball and kicks. It spirals high, long, and straight.

| | |
|---|---|
| **Coach Barnes:** | Nice kick! Who is that boy? |
| **Gym teacher:** | Joe? Nice kid. Quiet mostly. |
| **Coach Barnes:** | Do you think he can kick the ball like that again? |
| **Gym teacher:** | Let's watch and see. |
| **Narrator 3:** | A few minutes later, Joe catches the ball again. |
| **Narrator 1:** | Joe's kick is once again right down the middle, over the heads of the other team but well within bounds. |
| **Narrator 2:** | After class, the coach approaches Joe. |
| **Coach Barnes:** | Hey Joe, where did you learn to kick like that? |
| **Joe:** | In the street. You have to kick right down the middle or the ball bounces off parked cars. People hate that. |
| **Coach Barnes:** | *(laughing)* Yeah, I guess they would. Ever think of going out for football? |
| **Joe:** | Me? *(shakes his head)* Nah, sports isn't my thing. |
| **Coach Barnes:** | You've got a powerful kick. I'd like to see how you do punting and placekicking. Think about it. |
| **Joe:** | I don't know. I can't compete with those guys. |
| **Coach Barnes:** | You don't know until you try. Come by practice on Monday. We'll talk more. |

# Scene 2

| | |
|---|---|
| **Narrator 3:** | Arjun, Chelsea, and Joe have formed a band. Every Saturday afternoon they practice in Chelsea's father's garage. The band has never played in public, and the friends can't seem to agree on a name. |
| **Narrator 1:** | Joe finishes his can of soda and crunches the can. |
| **Joe:** | How about "Light Metal"? |
| **Chelsea:** | That's not the kind of music we play. |
| **Narrator 2:** | Joe tosses his empty soda can into the recycling bin. |
| **Joe:** | How about "The Recyclables"? |
| **Chelsea:** | But we don't recycle music. We make our own. I have a suggestion. How about "The Fringe"? |

| | |
|---|---|
| **Arjun:** | Fringe? Isn't that like lace or something? |
| **Chelsea:** | No, I mean like "On the Fringe." It means we're different. We're not like other bands. |
| **Joe:** | Like outsiders? |
| **Chelsea:** | No, not outsiders exactly. But not insiders either. |
| **Joe:** | And that's good? |
| **Chelsea:** | Well, sure it is. If you're on the inside, you only see the inside. If you are on the outside, you only see the outside. But if you're on the fringe. . . |
| **Arjun:** | *(guessing)* You see both sides? |
| **Chelsea:** | Exactly! |
| **Joe:** | "The Fringe." I like it. |
| **Arjun:** | Now all we need is someone to play for. |
| **Chelsea:** | I have an idea! Why don't we record our own CD? |
| **Joe:** | Wow. A CD? That's great. But doesn't that cost money? |
| **Chelsea:** | It doesn't if your dad works for a radio station. And mine does! He said he could help us. We can start recording next Saturday. But we have to practice really hard. Like after school every night this week, okay? |
| **Narrator 3:** | The boys agree to the plan. Chelsea crashes her cymbals in celebration. |

# Scene 3

| | |
|---|---|
| **Narrator 1:** | On Monday, the English teacher returns the class compositions. Joe stares at the red "C" on the top of his paper. Also in red is the teacher's comment: "You can do better." |
| **Narrator 2:** | Joe stares at the comment. He has always done just enough to get by. But Friday after gym class— well, he really liked hearing that he was good at something. |
| **Narrator 3:** | Joe replays his conversation with the coach in his head, all through the rest of English class. |

**Narrator 1:** By the time the bell rings, he has made a decision. He wants to be good at something.

**Narrator 2:** And if it isn't history or English, then maybe football is his thing after all. And so after school on Monday . . .

**Coach Barnes:** Hey, Joe! Glad you showed up. Listen up, boys. This is Joe Galván. I think he's going to be our new kicker.

**Joe:** I am? I mean, I thought we had to talk about it.

**Connor:** We don't talk football, Joe! We *play* football.

**Narrator 3:** He puts his arm over Joe's shoulder, welcoming him. Joe steps onto the field.

# Scene 4

**Narrator 1:** On Tuesday, Chelsea waits for Joe at his locker.

**Chelsea:** Where were you yesterday?

**Joe:** Oh, the band! I forgot.

**Chelsea:** How could you forget when it's so important?

**Joe:** I don't know. I just did, that's all.

**Chelsea:** You'll be there tonight, though, right?

**Joe:** I don't know for sure, Chelsea. I may be late.

**Chelsea:** What's the matter, Joe? Don't you want to make the CD?

**Joe:** Yeah, sure. But what's the rush?

**Chelsea:** My dad can give us time at the station, and I thought we could practice every night this week. . . .

**Joe:** I can't come on Friday. I have to be somewhere else.

**Chelsea:** Where?

**Joe:** *(quietly)* I have a football game.

**Chelsea:** What?

**Joe:** *(louder)* I have a football game on Friday night.

**Chelsea:** But you don't play football.

**Joe:** I do now. I joined the team, okay?

**Chelsea:** *(laughing)* You? Joe, you're not a jock.

**Joe:** *(hurt)* What do you know? Maybe I *am* a jock. I'm good, too! The guys all think so.

**Chelsea:** The "guys"? So, that's it? That's the end of "The Fringe"?

# *Scene 5*

---

**Narrator 2:** On Wednesday, Joe makes his way through the cafeteria with his lunch tray.

**Connor:** *(shouting)* Hey, Joe and his magic foot! Come sit with us!

**Narrator 3:** In the center of the cafeteria is a table where several members of the football team are eating lunch. Joe's a member of the team now. He likes the guys. They're fun to be with. Not just anyone gets to sit at that table.

**Narrator 1:** But across the room—near the exit door—are Chelsea and Arjun. He has sat with them at that table all year.

**Narrator 2:** Joe walks toward Arjun and Chelsea.

**Chelsea:** Lucky you! Being invited to sit with the cool guys.

**Joe:** Who said they're the cool guys?

**Chelsea:** Oh, admit it, Joe. You like being one of them.

**Joe:** *(sitting down)* How's the CD coming?

**Chelsea:** How do you think it's coming? We don't have a bass player! *(She gets up and walks away.)*

**Joe:** *(to Arjun)* She wants me to just play music—not football. Why can't I play both?

**Arjun:** We were counting on you, Joe.

**Joe:** So are they. I've got practice all week and a game on Friday.

**Arjun:** Chelsea's dad needs to know when we'll be ready to use his studio.

**Joe:** So, *you* think I should choose, too? You or them?

**Arjun:** Why do you even want to play football?

**Joe:** I'm not sure I do, but I like how it feels to be really good at something for once.

**Arjun:** You're a good bass player. *(pauses)* Oh well, you've got to do what you've got to do. *(getting up)* Good luck in the game, Magic Foot. We'll be cheering for you.

# Scene 6

**Narrator 3:** On Friday evening, parents and students fill the stands. Joe sees Arjun and Chelsea standing apart from the crowd, on the fringe.

**Narrator 1:** In the fourth quarter, the game is a scoreless tie with just three seconds on the clock. There is only enough time for one more play. Everyone looks over at Joe.

**Narrator 2:** Joe runs onto the field. All that counts now is kicking the ball through those goalposts. The ball is snapped to the holder. Joe's foot sends the ball through the posts and over the crossbar. The clock runs out. Joe's field goal wins the game.

**Narrator 3:** The team jumps around him, pounding his shoulder pads. Joe has never been in the middle of so much commotion.

**Connor:** Joe and his magic foot! What a kick! That was great!

**Narrator 1:** Joe feels something new—something warm and happy inside his chest. He looks up at the stands.

**Joe:** *(saying to himself, surprised)* They're cheering for me! No one's ever cheered for me before! Wow!

**Narrator 2:** Then Joe realizes that this—fans cheering—is exactly what Chelsea and Arjun and he had imagined . . . if they can ever make it as a band.

**Narrator 3:** He looks for Chelsea and Arjun in the crowd, but he does not see them now.

# Scene 7

**Narrator 1:** Thirty minutes later, Joe stands in front of Connor's house, where a victory party is being held. He can hear the guys talking about the game and laughing. Music comes from the open windows.

**Narrator 2:** That moment on the field, with everyone cheering— that was the best. It was the kind of cheers he and Arjun and Chelsea imagined they'd hear one day when they played on stage.

**Connor:** Hey, Magic Foot! You coming in?

**Joe:** You know, I'd like to, but I promised some friends I'd stop by. They're counting on me.

**Connor:** Well, you sure pulled through for us today!

**Narrator 3:** Joe waves goodbye and walks across town to Chelsea's garage. He hears Chelsea drumming.

**Narrator 1:** Joe grins and opens the door to join them.

**Joe:** Sorry I'm late.

**Chelsea:** Joe! You came! But what about football?

**Joe:** *(smiling)* What about it? Don't you think there's more to life than football?

**Arjun:** You didn't quit the team? Not after that field goal!

**Joe:** No, but I didn't quit the band, either. That is, if you guys still want me.

**Chelsea, Arjun:** Yes!

**Joe:** Okay, then. So, are we going to talk music or play music?

**Chelsea:** We're going to play. We have a CD to make.

**The End**

---

# *Think It Over*

1. Why does Joe think he is just an average guy? Do you agree with Joe's opinion of himself? Explain why or why not.

2. What changes Joe's life more—the coach telling him he is a good kicker or the teacher writing on Joe's paper that he could "do better"? Or does something else happen to make a bigger difference than either of these two things? Provide reasons to support your answer.

3. Chelsea tells Joe that he's not a jock. What does she mean by this? In your opinion, is she correct to assume this?

4. Are Chelsea and Arjun being understanding when they ask Joe to choose either football or the band? Why do they want him to choose?

5. How might this story have ended if Joe had missed the field goal that won the game?

# The Dancers

Rachel is nervous about performing in public, but she loves to dance. Although her father disapproves, Rachel auditions for the Youth Dance Competition. In the wings, however, is a girl who is determined to make Rachel embarrass herself so that the girl's best friend can steal the spotlight.

## Characters:

**Narrators 1, 2, 3**

**Rachel Land**, a seventh-grade dance student

**Olivia Benedict**, another dance student

**Amy Simmons**, Olivia's injured dance partner

**Aaron Land**, Rachel's older brother

**Mr. Land**, Rachel's father

**Director**

**Mrs. Benedict**, Olivia's mother

**Narrator 1:** An excited crowd of young people and their parents have gathered in the auditorium of the Community Arts Center. The auditions for the annual Youth Dance Competition are about to begin.

**Narrator 2:** The judges sit in the front row of seats. They will select 12 acts to perform on stage on the night of the competition.

**Narrator 3:** Last year, Amy and Olivia's tap dance duet took first place in the dance competition. This year, however, Amy has a broken ankle. Although Amy can't compete, she has come along tonight to cheer for Olivia.

**Narrator 1:** After her audition, Olivia sits in the seat next to Amy.

**Olivia:** How did I do? It's a little scary up there without you.

**Amy:** You are going to win it all. I just know it.

**Olivia:** I almost didn't come at all tonight. But my mother pushed me.

**Amy:** Omigosh! Look who's over there! Aaron Land! I'll bet he's going to audition. He's a great dancer.

**Olivia:** Who's that with him?

**Amy:** His sister Rachel.

**Olivia:** Maybe she's the one who is here to perform.

**Amy:** Oh, please! She never takes her nose out of a book.

**Narrator 2:** A few minutes later, the director calls the next performer to the stage.

**Director:** Number 11 is Rachel Land. She is going to perform a ballet routine for us.

**Narrator 3:** Rachel steps to the center of the stage. She is wearing ballet slippers. She glances nervously to the right and the left.

**Director:** (*reading from a card*) This is the first time Rachel has auditioned for the dance competition. (*to Rachel*) Don't be nervous, Rachel. Good luck.

**Amy:** (*sarcastically*) Oh, *this* should be good!

**Olivia:** You don't know that! She might be really great.

**Narrator 1:** Rachel gets into position and lifts her arms. The music begins and she dances.

**Narrator 2:** The audition lasts two minutes. When Rachel's performance ends, her brother applauds loudly.

**Olivia:** She was good. I'll bet they'll put her in the competition.

**Narrator 3:** When all the auditions are over, the judges tally the scores. The director announces the names.

**Narrator 1:** Amy is squeezing Olivia's hand so tightly that Olivia cries out.

**Amy:** There are only two slots left. Why haven't they called your name?

**Olivia:** Gosh, Amy! You're more excited about this than I am.

**Director:** And the final two performers are . . . Olivia Benedict and Rachel Land.

# Scene 2

**Narrator 2:** At home, after the performance, Rachel tells her father that she has been chosen to perform in the Youth Dance Competition.

**Rachel:** I didn't think I'd be selected, but I was! And now, you have to sign this paper so I can compete. It gives them permission to publish my name in the program and in the newspapers.

**Mr. Land:** *(reads)* It says here that they will record all performances for possible broadcast on television. No, Rachel. I don't like this show business stuff. You're too young.

**Rachel:** But Dad, I'm a good dancer!

**Mr. Land:** It's more important to be a good student. I don't think you can do both. Maybe next year.

**Narrator 3:** Disappointed, Rachel returns to her room with the unsigned form. Her brother knocks on the door and steps inside.

**Aaron:** You were great this afternoon! I knew you would be.

**Rachel:** It doesn't matter whether I was good or not. Dad won't sign the permission form.

**Aaron:** Did he tell you why?

**Rachel:** I'm too young and it's more important for me to be a good student. *(angrily)* I want to do other things, too—just like everyone else.

**Aaron:** Did you tell him that?

**Rachel:** He wouldn't understand. He doesn't know that everyone at school thinks I'm a "brain."

**Aaron:** Is that what the other kids call you?

**Rachel:** *(quietly)* Sometimes.

**Aaron:** So, you entered this competition to be more popular?

**Rachel:** *(shrugs)* Maybe. I don't know. I just thought it might be fun.

**Aaron:** If it's that important to you, Rachel, I'll sign the form. I'm 18. That means I'm legally an adult!

**Rachel:** But Dad said no!

**Aaron:** I'll convince him. You just worry about your dance routine—and having fun.

# Scene 3

**Narrator 1:** During rehearsal at the arts center, Amy coaches her best friend on her performance.

**Amy:** It's not just about talent. It's also about appearance and attitude. You have to smile more at the judges.

**Olivia:** You sound just like my mother!

**Amy:** The first place prize is $500 and a chance to compete at the state finals! That's a big deal!

**Narrator 2:** Rachel is listening. She already feels guilty that her brother signed her permission form after her father told her she couldn't compete. Now Amy's words make her feel as if she was foolish to even think of trying to compete with such a talented and popular girl as Olivia.

**Amy:** *(excitedly)* I think you should wear your hair differently this year. And I can help you put on your make-up. What color is your costume?

**Rachel:** *(interrupting)* We have to wear a costume?

**Amy:** *(sarcastically)* Excuse me, this is a private conversation! And yes, you have to have a costume. *If* you want to win.

**Olivia:** *(to Rachel)* Don't pay any attention to Amy. She's just mad because she broke her ankle and can't compete.

**Rachel:** It's just that I've never done anything like this before!

**Olivia:** Oh, I have! Plenty of times. Ever since I was a kid, my mother has dragged me to dance lessons.

**Rachel:** Don't you like to dance?

**Olivia:** Sure. I just hate to compete. My mother keeps pushing me.

**Rachel:** My father is same way, except he pushes me to get good grades.

**Olivia:** I've got plenty of costumes. I could lend you one.

**Rachel:** No, I don't think my father would like that. And he'd never allow me to wear make-up.

**Director:** Listen up, dancers. We have 12 acts to present in just 60 minutes, so everything must be carefully timed. Be sure to give your music to the stage manager and then wait on stage.

**Narrator 3:** Olivia and Rachel leave Amy alone in the wings. Amy feels left out, and not just because her ankle is in a cast.

**Narrator 1:** Then she gets an idea—a way to ensure that Rachel Land doesn't steal the first place prize from her best friend.

# Scene 4

**Narrator 2:** On the night of the competition, Amy hands the stage manager a CD.

**Amy:** This is Rachel Land's music. She made a change.

**Narrator 3:** Meanwhile in the dressing room, Mrs. Benedict helps Olivia apply make-up and put on her costume. Amy, who has just had her cast removed and wants to be in on the action, is also in the dressing room.

**Narrator 1:** Rachel puts on her ballet slippers, glancing shyly at Olivia, whose costume is beautiful.

**Narrator 2:** Rachel knows her simple blue leotard and tights are not as dazzling as Olivia's costume.

**Rachel:** I don't think I can do this. What if they don't like me? What if they laugh at me?

**Amy:** Gosh, Rachel. You should have thought of that earlier. You could always tell the director that you don't feel well. They can't make you dance.

**Olivia:** Amy, you're making her feel worse! *(to Rachel)* You were great at the audition and you made it this far. I think you'll do a great job. It's not a popularity contest. Just be yourself. Don't worry about "them."

**Narrator 3:** The house lights dim. The crowd in the auditorium gets quiet. The curtain opens. The competition begins.

**Amy:** *(to Olivia)* Don't worry. I took care of everything. The first place prize is yours. Guaranteed!

**Olivia:** What are you talking about?

**Amy:** Wait and see.

# Scene 5

**Director:** *(to audience)* Our next talented young dancer is Rachel Land. Please welcome her.

**Narrator 1:** Rachel steps on stage. She gets into position, her arms raised. The music begins, but—

**Narrator 2:** It is not the music Rachel has chosen and rehearsed. She hesitates, looking into the wings and then at the stage manager.

**Olivia:** But that's not Rachel's music. That's *my* music!

**Amy:** I know!

**Olivia:** Amy! What did you do?

**Narrator 3:** Rachel stands frozen in the spotlight, unable to dance. Finally, she hurries off the stage, in tears.

**Director:** Sorry, ladies and gentlemen. Looks like we have a little case of spotlight jitters. Let's bring on our next performer, shall we? Please welcome Olivia Benedict.

**Olivia:** Amy, did you change Rachel's music? How could you do such a terrible thing?

**Amy:** I'm your best friend. I wanted you to win! I guess I never thought how horrible Rachel would feel.

**Director:** *(repeating)* Olivia Benedict!

**Narrator 1:** Olivia walks on stage. She stares at the audience. When the music begins, Olivia does not dance.

**Narrator 2:** Olivia motions to the stage manager to stop the music. She looks out at the audience and takes a deep breath.

**Olivia:** I've danced in this competition before and I know how scary it is. But that's not what happened to Rachel.

**Narrator 3:** Rachel, who has been standing alone in a corner backstage crying, moves closer to the curtain to hear what Olivia is saying.

**Olivia:** There was a mix-up with the music. That wasn't Rachel's music. It was mine. If it's okay, I'd like to give up my spot so that Rachel can have her chance.

**Narrator 1:** Olivia walks off stage. She goes to the stage manager and tells her to put Rachel's original CD on. Then she goes up to Rachel and gives her a hug.

**Olivia:** Go ahead, Rachel. You know you can do this!

**Narrator 2:** A moment later, Rachel walks onto the stage again. The audience applauds warmly.

**Narrator 3:** Rachel puts on a beautiful performance. When she takes her final bow, she is smiling widely.

**Narrator 1:** Rachel does not win. Olivia has been eliminated. Even so, they hug each other backstage. Rachel's brother comes backstage to congratulate her.

**Narrator 2:** Behind Aaron are Rachel's father and Olivia's mother. Both parents are beaming. Mr. Land has flowers for Rachel.

| | |
|---|---|
| **Rachel:** | Dad! You came? |
| **Mr. Land:** | Aaron told me you needed to prove yourself. You were great! I didn't realize how important this was to you. |
| **Olivia:** | *(to her mother)* I hope you're not disappointed in me that I didn't compete. |
| **Mrs. Benedict:** | Disappointed? Not at all, Olivia. I'm very proud of you. |
| **Narrator 3:** | Olivia looks at Amy, who is standing alone. The two girls know the truth—the mix-up was not a mistake. Amy holds her breath, wondering if Olivia will tell. |
| **Narrator 1:** | Olivia does not say anything, but she does not smile at Amy. |
| **Narrator 2:** | As the two families leave, Olivia and Rachel walk out together, knowing that this could be the start of a great friendship. Meanwhile, Amy follows behind, wondering how everything managed to turn out just the opposite from what she had planned. |

### The End

# Think It Over

1. Why does Olivia enter the dance competition? Why does Rachel enter the dance competition?

2. Think about what the three dancers—Olivia, Amy, and Rachel—have in common and what is different about them. Which dancer seems more like an outsider at the beginning of the play? Which seems more like an outsider by the end? Explain why you think so.

3. In scene 3, the narrator says, "Amy feels left out, and not just because her ankle is in a cast." Explain what the narrator means.

4. How might this story have been different if Amy were also dancing in the competition? How might it have been the same?

5. Why did Amy switch the music so Rachel's dance routine would be disrupted? What did Amy fail to understand about her friend Olivia?

6. The story ends with Amy following behind Rachel and Olivia. How do you think Olivia and Amy's relationship has changed? What do you think Amy must do to make things right?

# Your Turn

1. In "On the Fringe," Chelsea says that "on the fringe" means not being an insider or an outsider and that's a good thing. Do you agree or disagree with Chelsea? Write a short paragraph explaining what "on the fringe" means to you.

2. Rewrite the ending of "The Dancers," providing dialogue between the three dancers backstage. What would Olivia say to Amy? What might Amy say to Rachel?

# Glossary

**audition** A tryout or test

**duet** A musical or dance routine involving two performers

**field goal** A kick in football that scores three points

**fringe** The outer area of something; on the edge. The word can also mean out of the ordinary, not part of the "mainstream" of a group or culture

**goalposts** A pair of upright posts linked by a crossbar through which the ball must be kicked in order to score

**house lights** The lights in the area of a theater where the audience sits

**placekicking** Kicking the ball while it is held on the ground or on a tee. Kicking a field goal is one kind of placekicking

**punt** In football, a type of kick where the player drops the ball and kicks it before it reaches the ground

**recyclable** Something that can be reused or turned into something new

**routine** A fixed program or set of actions

# About the Author

Catherine Gourley is the author of the award-winning nonfiction series *Women's Images and Issues of the 20th Century: How Popular Culture Portrayed Women in the 20th Century*. She is the national director of Letters About Literature, a reading promotion program of the Center for the Book in the Library of Congress.